W9-AXT-702

To: _____

From: _____

Date: _____

Forever-Love

J. COUNTRYMAN

NASHVILLE

A Thomas Nelson Company

Copyright © 1996 by Word Publishing, Inc.

All rights reserved. No portion of this publication may be
reproduced, stored in a retrieval system or transmitted in any form by any means—
electronic, mechanical, photocopying, recording, or any other—
except for brief quotations in printed reviews,
without the prior written permission of the publisher.

All material in this volume originally appeared
in *Making Love Last Forever* by Gary Smalley,
© 1996 Gary Smalley, and is used by permission.

J. Countryman is a registered trademark.

A J. Countryman Book

Designed by Left Coast Design, Portland, Oregon
Interior illustrations by Cecil Rice

Compiled and edited by Terri Gibbs

ISBN: 0-8499-5449-5

Printed and bound in Hong Kong

Foreword

Will our love last forever? It is the hope of every starry-eyed bride and groom who clasp hands and say, "I do." Yet as so aptly described in the title of a best-selling book: *Men Are from Mars, Women Are from Venus.* The differences between you and your mate are wonderful—and yet maddening. So how do you maintain your love? That's what the principles in this book are all about—staying in love with your mate.

Love's best-kept secret is not change (or exchange) your spouse or change your job or change your address. It's change your own course. Even small changes in your behavior can lead to major changes in your life.

Do you want to know the deep satisfaction that comes from being in love? It's simple—choose to love life and love your mate. Is it really possible to marry and then see that starry-eyed love actually get better? Yes. It's your choice!

GARY SMALLEY

Forever-Love

knows the power of the gift of praise.

raise is such a great gift, and it's so easy to give. So look at the things that make your spouse and others unique, and develop the habit of praising them for those very things. It will bring out the best in them.

2

Forever-Love

remembers to romance.

Women love to feel connection with their spouses,
and nothing accomplishes this better than romance.
For some it is flowers, cards, or a small gift. . . .
Still others look to a night out on the town,
a concert, or dinner. Women respond to
romance, and most desire more of it.

Forever-Love

is renewed and energized by tender touch.

As a couple, work at giving each
other the time you need to relax,
talk, and listen to each other.

Forever-Love

is bonded by a shared personal faith in God.

A husband and wife can know each other

as they both turn to and know God—

heart to heart.

5

Forever-Love

digs up the pearl buried within every trial.

Every painful trial is like an oyster,
and there is a precious pearl—a personal benefit—
in every one. Every single one.

6

Forever-Love

makes—even schedules—time for talk.

Tell me about your world.

I'll tell you about mine.

Forever-Love

sees conflict as a doorway to greater intimacy and knowledge.

Through this disagreement, what new insights can we gain about us as a couple? How can this eventually draw us closer?

8

Forever-Love

respects another person's personal boundaries.

We want others to respect the thoughts
and values we have chosen that reflect our most
personal selves, the part of us that is unique
and special, like a fingerprint.

Forever-Love

isn't afraid to look inside and ask, "What
characteristics of mine do others find most irritating?"

One of the best ways to improve our relationships

is to bring balance to any of our traits that we've

neglectfully or subconsciously

pushed to an extreme.

Forever-Love

*doesn't go it alone, but welcomes the
fresh insight of other perspectives.*

*I've never met a couple doing really well

that hasn't had help from others in some way—

from extended family, friends, good marriage

books, or a qualified marriage counselor.*

Forever-Love

calls for courage to move beyond the status quo.

When we nurture a marriage verbally,

emotionally, physically, and spiritually,

we can watch the love and intimacy

and knowledge grow.

12

Forever-Love

is protected when it grows in a diversified garden.

If we devote ourselves first to those things that deserve top priority, we'll find we're able to enjoy the many other good things as well. They come as energy-boosters.

18

Forever-Love

thrives on flexibility.

In a mutually satisfying relationship

both people's needs are expressed,

and they have the flexibility

of give and take.

Forever-Love

*stays in touch with a woman's intuitive sense
of what this marriage needs.*

Wives are like building inspectors;

they see things that, if left unnoticed,

could damage the marriage in the future.

A husband does himself a real favor

if he listens to what his wife has to

say concerning their marriage.

15

Forever-Love

*is not so goal oriented that it loses sight
of relationship and connection.*

*If a woman feels safe, secure, loved,
and honored in her marriage, she will find it far
easier to get in touch with her needs and her
intuitive sense of how things are going.*

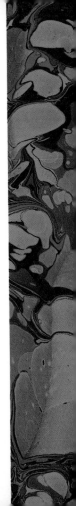

16

Forever-Love

knows that marital conflict is inevitable.

*The good news is that we can not only
reduce our conflicts, we can also use them to
move into deeper intimacy in any relationship.*

Forever-Love

makes a truelove feel safe.

In any healthy relationship, people have the freedom to think for themselves. We want our spouses to use their creativity and intelligence to complement our own.

Forever-Love

is honor put into action regardless of the cost.

onor goes hand in glove with love,

a verb whose very definition is doing worthwhile

things for someone who is valuable to us.

19

Forever-Love

highly values a truelove.
"With me, you carry weight!"

When we honor someone we give

that person a highly respected

position in our lives.

20

Forever-Love

*knows that good sex is a reflection
of a good relationship.*

*Verbal intercourse is vital to a healthy sex life.
It involves getting to know your mate
through conversation and
spending time together.*

21

Forever-Love

is doubly blessed by the contributions of
two unique personalities. It values variety.

*Natural tendencies that may be
fundamentally different from
your own can **enrich** you
and your marriage.*

Forever-Love

does not welcome anger as a heart-guest.

There's a major destroyer of love on the loose . . .

this destroyer is forgotten,

unresolved anger.

23

Forever-Love

assumes that things will get better, not worse.

All our trials, great and small,
can bring more of the two best things in life:
love for life and love for others.

24

Forever-Love

*never demands its own way but searches
for ways of enriching the other person.*

Oneness does not mean that one mate

dominates the other or that the stronger

controls the weaker.

Forever-Love

is not a genie. "Your wish" is not "my command."

$\mathcal{E}$ach one of us is a separate and unique

person—worthy of two kinds of respect.

(1) Respect from others.

(2) Respect from ourselves.

Forever-Love

believes that even small behavior changes can lead
to major improvements in relationships.

*Almost anyone can make small adjustments
if he or she believes it will make
a lasting positive difference.*

27

Forever-Love

knows the destructive, alienating power of anger.

*Anger is our choice. We can choose to see its
powerful potential for destruction and take the
steps to reduce it within us. Otherwise, it's
an iceberg sinking our love.*

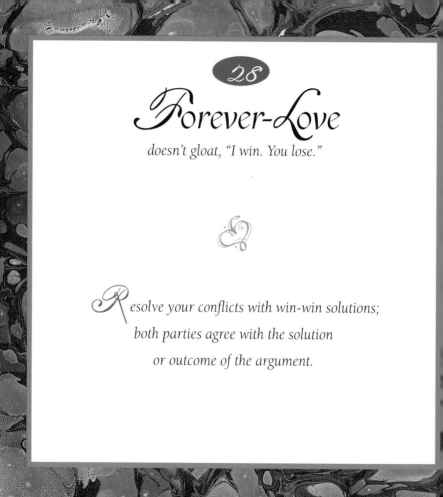

28

Forever-Love

doesn't gloat, "I win. You lose."

Resolve your conflicts with win-win solutions;
both parties agree with the solution
or outcome of the argument.

29

Forever-Love

*analyzes long-standing complaints
to find a core of truth.*

*Think of two or three main points of criticism
that have persisted for some time, write them down,
and look at what they actually reflect.*

30

Forever-Love

relies on God as its enduring source of power.

When we quit pretending that our spiritual journey doesn't matter, we're on our way to availing ourselves of the power we need to love life and others.

Forever-Love

*doesn't feel the need to "fix"
everything about everybody.*

*Better understanding of the motivations
and actions that grow out of our basic
personalities can help us achieve
personal and marital satisfaction.*

32

Forever-Love

asks, "How can our differences draw us together?"

*Our strengths complement each other
and make for a great team.*

Forever-Love

*freely expresses feelings in mutual,
nonthreatened self-disclosure.*

Sharing deep feelings with each other is

emotional intercourse, and it's vital

to sexual satisfaction.

34

Forever-Love

does not deny a grievance but grieves the harm's loss.

In dealing with your own anger,
it's best to face it. And don't cut short
your need to grieve.

35

Forever-Love

reaches out to share the joy of life.

As we reach out to another,

our own needs for fulfillment

and love are met.

Forever-Love

*knows the quiet, confident strength that
comes with self-respect.*

*Respect for others is half the boundary
issue; respect for self is the other
critical ingredient.*

Forever-Love

forms a private love language.

Both partners develop a list:

"These actions make me feel

loved and honored."

Forever-love reaches out and energizes a truelove

by suggesting a love-language activity.

Forever-Love

*steps out and makes adjustments
to "go for" a better relationship.*

*Enriching the life of another
is often more satisfying than doing
something for ourselves.*

Forever-Love

measures its criticism.

ive seven or more praises
for every one fault-finding suggestion.

Forever-Love

*approaches conflict saying,
"Let's work to resolve this issue so that
your needs and mine are met."*

*For a marriage to grow as a result of conflict
—for healing to occur after conflict—
we need to learn to move toward resolution.*

Forever-Love

says, "I love you," even when
a resolution isn't reached.

*C*ommitment and lasting love

has a way of softening the dispute.

Forever-Love

takes time for play. Foreplay.

You cannot lose by spending extra time touching, hugging, and cuddling your wife. Praise her, tell her how desirable she is, and give her spontaneous hugs.

44

Forever-Love

knows how to say "I'm sorry" and "I forgive you."

*A contrite spirit and gentle touch
start the healing and resolving process.*

45

Forever-Love

does not work to change or exchange a spouse.

Instead, it realizes, "If something's wrong,
it's up to me to change my response
and my mind-set."

Forever-Love

listens to the heart's warnings—fear, frustration, and hurt—and makes the choice to get better, not bitter.

After a hurtful, fearful, or frustrating experience, we can move in one of two directions: toward getting better or toward getting bitter.

Forever-Love

knows that meaningful communication takes time.

*Slow down and discuss decisions
with your spouse; don't just charge
ahead on your own.*

48

Forever-Love

steers clear of manipulative, subtle criticism.

*Criticism drills a hole in our emotions,
and through that hole our energy flows
out. Along with it goes most of
our motivation to try to do better.*

49

Forever-Love

looks for attributes and actions to praise.

*ow do you bring out the best in
your mate? Give the gift of praise.
The impact can be monumental.*

50

Forever-Love

*does not tune out or get defensive in
the face of constructive suggestions for
improving the relationship.*

*Asking, "How can we improve things between
us?" and listening respectfully to the answer,
takes the marriage in a healthful direction.*

51

Forever-Love

accepts the reality of the past but lives beyond the blame game.

I understand my past, but I'll be hanged before I will allow it to determine my future!

52

Forever-Love

can't change the weather.
It *can* choose how to respond to the weather.

You choose your own response to each situation.

You can decide to be persistent and hopeful.

If you do, I can almost guarantee your

future will be better than your past.

Forever-Love

*encourages conversation, listens well,
and values the words of others.*

In a good relationship,

you have not only the freedom to think,

but you are also encouraged to talk,

to express yourself.

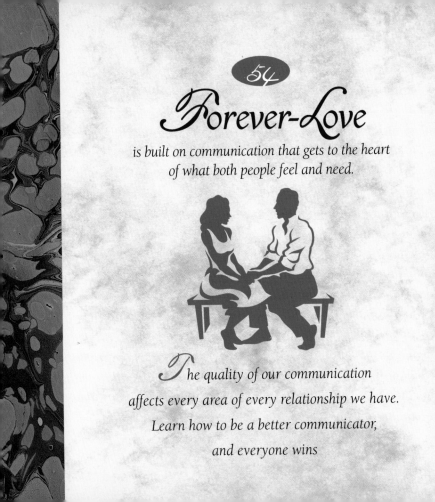

54

Forever-Love

is built on communication that gets to the heart
of what both people feel and need.

The quality of our communication

affects every area of every relationship we have.

Learn how to be a better communicator,

and everyone wins

55

Forever-Love

knows that life will never be perfect.

*Learn to relax,
and don't expect others
to do things just like you.*

56

Forever-Love

says, "Thanks. I needed that."

Heroic love sacrifices itself for the enrichment of the other. It doesn't seek its own good but chooses to satisfy the desires of the beloved.

Forever-Love

knows that power isn't in positions and titles.

*O*nly if I'm allowing God to meet my needs
and empower me with his love, joy, peace, and
contentment every day am I truly happy
regardless of my circumstances.

58

Forever-Love

admits its failures and asks for grace.

*When I'm aware of how I've missed God's mark
by acting in an unloving way, I seek his forgiveness.
That keeps our relationship open.*

59

Forever-Love

says, "I'll take responsibility for my
own choices—past, present, and future."

*Turn away from the blame game,
no matter how difficult your past has been,
and embrace the great, freeing truth
that **you will be as content
as you choose to be.***

60

Forever-Love

looks for ways to connect with a truelove.

*We build better connections with others
through shared experiences, intimate conversations,
meaningful touch, and shared crises.*

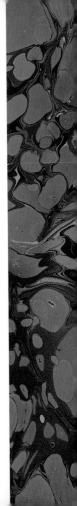

61

Forever-Love

seeks to identify an offense.

*N*ame a fear or a loss, and anger
begins to lose its debilitating power.

62

Forever-Love

tries to understand any "why"
behind another's hurtful actions.

*M*ake the effort to understand
the individual's background and motivation.
Let your new understanding of that person's pain
and life difficulty drain some of your anger.

Forever-Love

tempers temperamental extremes and cultivates the
strengths of less-dominant characteristics.

"*For you, my truelove, I'll rein myself
in and go for balance.*"

64

Forever-Love

inspects life—to compare expectations against reality.

The wider the gap between what we expect and the reality of what we experience, the greater the potential for discouragement and fatigue.

65

Forever-Love

says no to anger's misery and yes to inner freedom.

Unresolved anger and blame can imprison us and bind us and make us miserable at heart and miserable to live with.

66

Forever-Love

avoids extreme thoughts.

When you hit hard times,
try to refocus some of your energy
away from all that's bad and instead
search for anything that could possibly
be good in the trial you're facing.

67

Forever-Love

gives a wound time to heal.

*As you dig into your tribulations
and discover the gems buried within them,
your self-worth will soar, and so will your
ability to give and receive love.*

68

Forever-Love:

Use it or lose it.

When we face hardship,
we don't have to get bitter.
We can choose to use the hardship
to make love grow bigger and better.

Forever-Love

says the future = hope.

Accept the reality of the past while choosing to live beyond it. Take responsibility for your own future choices.

70

Forever-Love

tries to view a situation through the eyes of a truelove.

Try to "get inside your truelove's mind."
*Start saying the things you imagine he or she would
say; you'll be amazed at the insights that come.*

Forever-Love

doesn't ask the impossible of a truelove:
"Be my power-pack."

I'm going to stop relying on people

or my job for fulfillment. I recognize that God's

creation can't ultimately give me the kind of

contentment that only God can give.

72

Forever-Love

*measures words carefully and only makes
requests that are within the realm of reason.*

The key to deep verbal intimacy
is feeling safe to share our feelings and needs
and sensing that our feelings and needs
are valued by our mate.

Forever-Love

equally respects self and others.

*Clearly defining who we are is essential.
It can make or break our love for life and the
satisfaction we receive from relationships
built on respect and honor.*

Forever-Love

tempers the aggressive and strengthens the passive.

*For people who tend to be too aggressive or too passive the final word is **moderation**.*

Forever-Love

does not belittle the feelings of others.

*In a healthy relationship, you know
your thoughts and words will be valued.
You have the freedom to share your feelings,
knowing they will be respected.*

Forever-Love

gives God the highest value in life.

*As we experience God meeting our needs
and doing things that could only be described as
miraculous, we gain a peace and happiness
that's beyond what we had imagined
gaining from other people.*

Forever-Love

*does not see doom in every gap
between expectations and reality.*

*I*f the two of you discover that your
expectations and experience don't match up
well in a particular area of your life, you need to
determine whether you should try to change the
expectations or the reality (or both).

Forever-Love

chooses to forgive—to untie the knot
of anger and release the bitter blame.

The original definition of **forgiveness**
actually means that you untie or release someone.
Being untied involves a conscious and deliberate
release of the offender through an act of forgiveness.

Forever-Love

looks for things to agree on.

There is terrific strength and consistency

when you are united on a course of

action that you both believe in

and are committed to.

Forever-Love

*chooses to appreciate the qualities that
make each person different from the other.*

*As you learn to understand various
differences between you and your spouse,
you can spark appreciation for qualities
he or she has that you lack.*

Forever-Love

expresses energizing praise—anytime, anywhere.

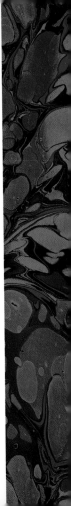

Try praising your spouse and see what happens.

Praise is like a shot of adrenaline

that energizes a person.

82

Forever-Love

resolves today's conflicts today—not tomorrow.

Conflicts have the potential for drawing you and your spouse closer to each other. It's a matter of opening the door to intimacy— not closing it, slamming it, or locking it.

Forever-Love

*considers the long-term effects of decisions
when conflict is otherwise deadlocked.*

Sorting out the big issues is a practical

approach to reaching resolution.

Forever-Love

"deposits" more than it "withdraws."

*A **deposit** is anything positive, security-producing. It's a gentle touch, a listening ear, a fun, shared experience. A **withdrawal** is anything sad or negative. It's a harsh word, an unkept promise.*

Forever-Love

asks for feedback. "What energizes
or drains energy from you?"

*I*f you make no deposit, you'll get no return.
Make deposits and you not only energize your
spouse, you energize your marriage and your own life.

86

Forever-Love

is energized as one person takes a step to
renew the other and the relationship.

*Enthusiasm—for life, for romance,
for "us"—is contagious.*

Forever-Love

sex thrives on variety within monogamy.

The sexual relationship is a place where creativity should shine. Sex was never meant to be dull, boring, or routine.

Forever-Love

"goes for connection" on four levels:
verbal, emotional, physical, and spiritual.

Good sex has four equally important
elements—and only one of them is physical.

89

Forever-Love

is handicapped by too much distance
between partners and/or too much control
by one over the other.

In a healthy relationship each person

feels valued, cared for, safe, and loved.

Each person is relatively content with life

and is growing toward maturity.

Forever-Love

does not charge ahead, making unilateral decisions.

People who push their strong, decisive
leadership qualities too far can become overbearing,
hyperaggressive, domineering people who trample
anyone who gets in their way.

Forever-Love

takes the risk to ask, "What are you feeling right now?"

❦

We can reach the deeper levels of loving and being loved only when we put ourselves at risk of having our feelings misunderstood or ridiculed.

92

Forever-Love

allows others to think for themselves.

We want our spouses to use their creativity and intelligence to complement our own. Like someone once said, "If both of us think exactly alike, one of us is unnecessary."

Forever-Love

*thrives on shared, minor crises that,
when remembered, prompt laughter.*

*Any shared crises can bring you and your
mate into a deeper sense of closeness. The key is
to go through the crises together however
and whenever they happen.*

94

Forever-Love

is not afraid to ask for help
to break bad habits learned in childhood.

*W*hen the people we love begin helping
us love them more, they are usually much more
tolerant of our ways and forgiving of us.

95

Forever-Love

strives for self-control
but knows the grace of self-forgiveness.

*D*on't deny your dominant temperament

but do temper your natural tendencies.

96

Forever-Love

can hold its ground against intimidation.

As you claim your ground, speak in love. Speak with respect for yourself and the other person. Be reasonable but firm.

Forever-Love

looks beyond disagreement and conflict
to identify what needs are begging to be met.

$\mathcal{A}$s soon as we are in conflict,

we have to open a door so we can

walk through it to find out what the

other person feels and needs.

Forever-Love

thinks in terms of teamwork, accentuating the strengths of both partners that can "cover" the weaknesses of either.

We want people to respect who we are and see us as separate from them— but also as a loving part of them.

99

Forever-Love

asks permission before entering someone's garden.

*You have the ability to set boundaries
and ask that they be maintained.*

Forever-Love

doesn't make impossible demands,
and it accepts the reality that a truelove
is not an all-sufficient god or parent.

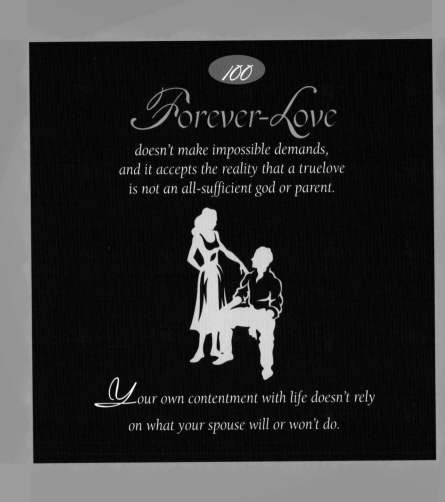

Your own contentment with life doesn't rely

on what your spouse will or won't do.

Forever-Love

*sets down fighting rules— boundaries
that aren't to be crossed.*

*If conflict is going to draw a couple
closer together, they need a list of fighting rules.
Without such boundaries, you may say or do things
that shut down communication—that
slam the door on intimacy.*

102

Forever-Love

*maintains energy as it is challenged
through loving, supportive accountability.*

*Meeting with a support group regularly,
encouraging each other and being encouraged
that you're not alone in your efforts to make
a better marriage can be tremendously energizing.*

Forever-Love

doesn't go looking for a fight
just to find the joy of making up.

We **need** to have disagreements,

but we don't go looking for fights.

104

Forever-Love

*communication creates a thirst—piques
an interest—for "tell me more."*

*D*on't try to make your point until you

have someone's full, undivided attention.

To get that attention, pique that person's

interest until he or she is

motivated to listen.

105

Forever-Love

*is not so desperate to please
that it says yes to every request.*

*The ability to say no can help you set the
boundaries essential for your
own well-being.*

Forever-Love

weighs the consequences of words and
actions and doesn't lash out when under stress.

Develop sensitivity to the feelings of others

and weigh the consequences of your words or

actions before jumping into something.

Forever-Love

communication uses vivid word pictures
to make it easy for a true-love to
understand feelings and needs.

*W*ord pictures help us "step into the other
person's shoes" and experience something emotionally
close to what he or she feels.

108

Forever-Love

knows that natural temperament doesn't
need to control life's temperature.
"I can temper my control."

*Focus on ways you can improve
your marriage by making yourself
easier to live with.*

Forever-Love

*doesn't jump to the conclusion that
a truelove is intentionally trying to exasperate.*

*Usually the behavior that frustrates us is just a
reflection of the way our spouse is. He or she is not
trying to strain the marriage but is just being natural.*

Forever-Love

*is courageous enough to ask,
"What would make this relationship better?"*

*As you increase your understanding
of your complementary strengths you'll have more
ammunition with which to praise your mate.*

III

Forever-Love

resists the temptation to psychologize
or make blanket assumptions about a truelove's
motives or reasons for behavior.

Look for the positive; discover the value of variety!

Forever-Love

*finds courage to break out of
long-standing, circular fight patterns.*

*We're not doomed to an endless cycle
of unresolved conflict. If you're stuck on a
merry-go-round, you'll need to take the risk
of stepping out of old patterns.*

Forever-Love

hears "no" or "not now" with grace—not with paranoia.

Ask permission before entering someone else's "space" and then be willing to accept the answer you're given, even if it's not the one you wanted.

Forever-Love

*doesn't clam up and shut down
in the face of verbal conflict.*

*Use conflict as a doorway to intimacy,
to get past opinions to feelings. Conflict used in
this way is actually a good thing that moves
the relationship forward.*

Forever-Love

identifies and nurtures five priority concerns.

If we have five priority areas
and a problem develops in one or two of them
our health in the other areas can lift our spirits
and restore our energy. Diversify. Give
*attention to **all** five areas.*

Forever-Love

*reduces life-strain by closing the
gap between expectations and reality.*

*Slow down and give your life a reality check.
How do your expectations compare
to your life's realities?*

Forever-Love

*communication repeats back
what has been heard and then asks,
"Have I understood your message and motive?"*

*Repeat your message until the
individual gets it right. This method can
be especially effective when you're
communicating feelings or needs.*

Forever-Love

*doesn't feel compelled to give in and
maintain peace at any price.*

*When one person wins because the other
one gives in, peace prevails for a season but the
other person loses and ultimately
the relationship also loses.*

Forever-Love

is possible, no matter what your circumstances.

It's perfectly normal for a marriage to go through different seasons—of drought, worry, sadness, anger and also times of plenty, happiness, and overwhelming joy and laughter.

Epilogue . . .

When a husband and wife both want their partner
to receive life's best before they do,
you have a marriage that's going
to exceed every wedding-day dream.
This love not only lasts,
it continually grows.